FPI Case Studies
Number 14

THE UNITED STATES AND THE LAW OF THE SEA TREATY

Steven R. David
Peter Digeser

FPI Foreign Policy Institute
The Paul H. Nitze
School of Advanced International Studies
The Johns Hopkins University
Washington, D.C.

Library of Congress Cataloging-in-Publication Data

David, Steven R.
The United States and the Law of the
Sea Treaty / Steven R. David, Peter Digeser.
p.   cm. — (FPI case studies ; no. 14)
1. Maritime law—United States.   2. United States—
Foreign relations—1945–   . 3. Maritime law.
I. Digeser, Peter.   II. Title.   III. Series.
JX4422.U5D38   1989
341.4'5'0973—dc20   89–22366 CIP

ISBN 0–941700–54–2 (pbk. : alk. paper)

Distributed by arrangement with

University Press of America, Inc.
4720 Boston Way
Lanham, MD 20706/ (301) 459-3366

3 Henrietta Street
London, WC2E 8LU
England

About the Authors

Steven R. David is associate professor of political science at The Johns Hopkins University in Baltimore. His interests are in Superpower-Third World relations.

Peter Digeser is assistant professor of political science at the University of California at Santa Barbara. His research interests lie in twentieth-century political philosophy.

THE JOHNS HOPKINS
FOREIGN POLICY INSTITUTE

The Johns Hopkins Foreign Policy Institute (FPI) was founded in 1980 and serves as the research center for the The Paul H. Nitze School of Advanced International Studies (SAIS) in Washington, D.C. The FPI is a meeting place for SAIS faculty members and students as well as for government analysts, policymakers, diplomats, journalists, business leaders, and other specialists in international affairs. In addition to conducting research on policy-related international issues, the FPI sponsors conferences, seminars, and roundtables.

Current research activities at the FPI span the complete spectrum of American foreign policy and international affairs. FPI programs examine the future of U.S.-Soviet relations; the impact of the landmark Goldwater-Nichols defense reorganization act; the relation of arms control to force structure and military-political doctrine; the politics of international terrorism; the role of the media in foreign policy; American and Soviet national security policymaking; and other leading international issues. These programs are usually directed by FPI fellows.

In addition to books and monographs, FPI publications include the *SAIS Review*, a semiannual journal of foreign affairs, which is edited by SAIS students; the FPI Policy Briefs, a series of analyses of immediate or emerging foreign-policy issues; the FPI Case Studies, a series designed to teach analytical negotiating skills; the FPI Policy Consensus Reports, which present recommendations on a series of critical foreign policy issues; and the SAIS Energy papers, presenting new research on energy resource issues.

For additional information regarding FPI activities, write to: FPI Publications Program, The Paul H. Nitze School of Advanced International Studies, The Johns Hopkins University, 1619 Massachusetts Avenue, N.W., Washington, D.C. 20036-2297.

Contents

Foreword

The Johns Hopkins Foreign Policy Institute (FPI) of the School of Advanced International Studies (SAIS) has been awarded support from The J. Howard Pew Freedom Trust for the development of twenty-five case studies on formal diplomatic negotiations. To promote the collegiality of this effort, and to fulfill the educational mission of the school and the institute, these cases are being developed primarily by SAIS faculty members and FPI fellows or research associates working together, in most instances, with a SAIS student. Students selected to participate in this project are usually Ph.D. or M.A. candidates. Their contribution is such as to warrant coauthorship.

These cases are being designed to be tested by their authors and their colleagues in the curriculum at SAIS. They are also made available for other institutions to use as part of their own teaching programs. Accordingly, they include teaching notes that can guide their adoption as a pedagogical tool. As explained by I. William Zartman, the program director, these cases form a scholarly endeavor designed to improve understanding of the diplomatic negotiation process and a pedagogical effort designed to permit the active transmission of that understanding.

The FPI was opened by SAIS in 1980 to provide the connection between the school's academic research and the real world of international policy questions. Nonpartisan and nonideological, the FPI is a place for individuals from diverse fields to debate and confer on a common goal: the formation of coherent U.S. responses to international events. The FPI organizes roundtables, conferences, lectures, and policy study groups. It sponsors research on current world problems and publishes papers and studies of interest to scholars and policymakers alike. The FPI chairman is Harold Brown, secretary of defense during the Carter administration.

We are especially grateful to The J. Howard Pew Freedom Trust for its generous support in the development of this program; to the many experts, including numerous current and former officials involved in these negotiations, for their willingness to help review the initial draft of these cases; to our colleagues at SAIS who, under the leadership of Dean George Packard, have shown such interest in this program as to agree to prepare these cases; and to our students, whose able participation is helping make this program successful.

Simon Serfaty
Executive Director

Introduction

This is one in a series of case studies of negotiation prepared as teaching materials by The Johns Hopkins Foreign Policy Institute (FPI) of the School of Advanced International Studies (SAIS) on a grant from The J. Howard Pew Freedom Trust. The project is designed to improve understanding—and the transmission of that understanding—of the diplomatic negotiation process. The cases are prepared for classroom use as an assist to teaching analytical negotiating skills, through presentation and discussion, and as comprehensive portrayals and analyses of specific instances of international negotiation.

As a teaching aid, the case studies are generally interrupted at turning points in the negotiation; the narrative stops and students are asked, "What would you do now?" The rest of the page is left blank, so that students and professors can discuss appropriate responses as participants in the situation. When positions and their implications are fully explored, the page can be turned to see what happened in reality, and the narrative continues. Reality has authority, but not exclusively so. It is important to understand why experienced negotiators acted as they did, and it is also important to examine alternative responses to find their implications and their impediments. Because of the complex nature of this case study, the authors have presented questions to student readers in an appendix.

Discussions at the break points can be conducted in one of two ways. As in the usual case method of teaching, they can simply be open discussions, with the teacher acting as Socratic questioner and moderator. Discussants should focus on exploring courses of action that are both innovative and realistic and on examining their implications. The emphasis should be on personal, operational responses. An alternative is to assign roles and proceed to simulation on the basis of the case narrative. The advantage lies in the allocation and division of responsibilities. In many cases the key to the outcome lies as much in the composition of each side and its intra-party negotiations as in the negotiations between the established parties. Roles should be assigned to represent component interests and agencies, and a spokesman should be appointed for the collective party.

The cases are structured on a simple, but useful, framework for analyzing the negotiation process. This case begins with a brief background summary and then focuses on regime change. Negotiations are necessary when there is a need to change an international regime or an understood set of practices and norms governing a particular relationship. As previous arrangements break down and new relations are required, the issue to be resolved becomes increasingly clear and forms the agenda for the negotiations. This section indicates the previous regime, the reason for its breakdown, and the way in which salient issues developed and brought themselves to the attention of the negotiating parties. The third section looks at the interests, power, and parties involved. The fourth section discusses precipitants that brought about negotiations and the conditions that made the moment particularly ripe for negotiations.

In the next sections the narrative focuses on process, beginning with prenegotiations. Although this aspect is usually neglected in studies of face-to-face negotiations, it forms a necessary part of the process, as participants diagnose the problem and issues and develop an understanding of the other party's position. This stage culminates in a decision on whether to negotiate, based on a perception of the problem's susceptibility to solution by negotiation, but diagnosis also continues as the negotiation proceeds (and sometimes takes place only once formal negotiations have begun).

The next stage in the process is the search for a formula, that is, a common understanding of the problem or agreed terms of trade for its solution. Although the search for a formula is not always explicit, it is usually present. The case study identifies the proposed formulas and indicates the strategies by which a common formula for solution was achieved, including the decision to leave out any insoluble problems. Included in this discussion is an identification of turning points, or crises, when the parties broke off negotiations before returning to resolve the issue.

The process continues as parties implement their formula by working out the details of the agreement while proceeding to closure rather than continuing to discuss. Without indicating every detail and all the tactics involved in reaching an agreement, this section shows the general areas of detail, the way in which parties implemented the formula, and the tactics and decisions involved in ending negotiations at a mutually satisfactory point, even though the settlement was only partial and temporary.

A guide to teaching the study is available separately on request. It includes a section on leverage that not only focuses on the elements of power identified with the parties but evaluates specific moments of pressure that were effective. The teaching notes also draw lessons for negotiation behavior.

We expect that the case study framework will provide the basis for students to understand the negotiation process and that it will stimulate greater creativity by negotiations.

I. William Zartman
Program Director

Background

I f the aspirations of the participants at the third United Nations Conference on the Law of the Sea (UNCLOS III) were considerable, so were the impediments to arriving at a treaty. UNCLOS III aspired not only to settle and codify traditional maritime issues but to preempt international conflict over the resources on the deep-seabed floor. The fulfillment of these hopes meant negotiating a treaty from an enormous agenda, in a worldwide forum, over an extended period of time. The negotiating agenda included issues not only of overflight, navigation, and fishing but of scientific experimentation, property, resource recovery, and sovereignty. Moreover, because these issues were discussed in a forum that included more participants than the United Nations, the process of arriving at a treaty would require satisfying a diverse and hostile set of factions. Every issue confronted the different interests of yet another group of states. In addition, because of the extended duration of the negotiations, interests differed not only between states but within states. Within this dynamic environment negotiators attempted to codify the law of the sea.

This case study begins with the Nixon administration's decision to submit a proposal for the law of the sea in August 1970 (although the UN Seabed Committee had been active since the late 1960s). The first formal negotiating session of UNCLOS III was held in June 1974; the final session was held in April 1982. During the first period, which ended in 1975, the negotiations outlined a settlement for many traditional maritime issues. Much of the remaining time was devoted to questions regarding the deep-seabed and international boundaries. From the American perspective, the central issue during the first period was what kind of regime would best satisfy U.S. coastal and maritime interests. In the second period, the central issue was what kind of international regime should govern the exploration and exploitation of manganese nodules lying on the ocean floor.

Did the law of the sea negotiations successfully deal with these issues? This question has no simple answer, particularly from the American perspective. Although a comprehensive and universally acceptable treaty was not achieved, the negotiating process may have advanced U.S. interests. At the very least, UNCLOS III illustrated the problems of conducting large-scale multilateral negotiations over an extended period of time.

Regime Change

U NCLOS III can be seen, in part, as a response to the erosion of the regime of freedom of the seas. The origins of this regime can be traced to the challenge of the English and the Dutch to Portuguese and Spanish hegemony over the oceans. This challenge, defended by Hugo Grotius in his tract, *Mare Liberum* (1618), argued for the right to navigate and fish freely. In the following two hundred years the emergent regime, supported by British naval power, sought to guarantee high seas freedoms and the right to innocent passage through territorial waters.[1] Since 1945, however, the efficacy of that regime has increasingly come into doubt.

The historical alternative to the regime of the freedom of the seas has been characterized by enclosure. As advocated by John Selden in *Mare Clausam* (1635), this alternative divided the seas in much the

---

[1]Because many of the traditional issues of maritime law relate to the placement of boundary lines, it is helpful to have some familiarity with the various boundaries drawn under international law. The first of these is the *baseline*. The baseline provides the point at which other maritime boundaries are drawn. The waters enclosed by this line are *internal waters*, to which other states have no general rights. In contrast, outside the baseline other states do enjoy certain general rights. The baseline does *not* mark the outer limit of the state's territory. This brings us to the next boundary, which establishes the *territorial sea*. Under international law, the territorial sea is also part of the state's territory and during the freedom of the seas regime extended three miles from the baseline into the ocean (which was roughly the range of a cannon in the eighteenth century). In UNCLOS III the territorial sea was extended to twelve miles. Although states exercise sovereignty in this zone, other states retain certain rights (for example, innocent passage). The boundary of the next zone, the *contiguous zone*, is twenty-four miles from the baseline (twelve miles from the territorial sea boundary). Within this zone a state may exercise its enforcement and legislative powers in fiscal, immigration, or sanitation matters. UNCLOS III also established an *Exclusive Economic Zone* (EEZ), which extends two hundred miles from the baseline. The coastal state enjoys extensive rights to natural resources on the seabed and in the superjacent waters within the EEZ. Coastal states also have economic rights to the continental shelf, even if it extends beyond two hundred miles. In the EEZ, outside states have rights to navigate, fly over, and lay cable and pipeline. Beyond the EEZ lie the *high seas*, which no state may subject to its sovereignty but in which all states may exercise the rights to navigate, fly over, fish, lay pipeline, and so on. Generally, enforcement of these rights on the high seas are left to the flag state (that state which has granted the ship the right to sail under its flag).

same way that land would be divided: the jurisdiction of a state would extend across the ocean until it met the jurisdiction of another state. In the twentieth century the pressures for enclosure have been expressed in calls for increasing the width of the territorial sea and creating some kind of special-purpose contiguous zones over which the coastal state would have exclusive economic or scientific rights. Although these pressures were manifest prior to World War II, they have become increasingly powerful in the last four decades. It should be noted, however, that such pressures are not new phenomena. As far back as ancient Greece and Rome, the forces of enclosure have competed with desires for establishing freedom of the seas.

In modern times the primary challenge to the freedom of the seas regime has come in the form of unilateral claims for ocean resources. The most significant of these claims were the Truman proclamations of 1945, which asserted the right of the United States to the resources beneath the continental shelf and created a national fishing conservation zone. However, the proclamations claimed jurisdiction neither to the continental shelf itself nor to the superjacent waters. Although limited in nature, the Truman proclamations provided a fertile precedent for unilateral claims by other countries. Because the jurisdictional claims of the Truman administration were based simply on "physical adjacency and anticipation of use,"[2] they provided a justification for other nations to make much broader claims. Between 1945 and 1950 thirty nations asserted rights to the continental shelf or some form of contiguous zone. Many of these claims were made by Central and South American countries, which created maritime or national zones as wide as 200 miles. Such unilateral moves persisted through the 1950s and 1960s.

A number of reasons can be offered to explain the increasing pressures for enclosure. Many of these involve technological imperatives. The years following World War II saw an increase in offshore drilling capabilities, an improved ability to locate, catch, and process fish, and the beginnings of the technology to recover manganese nodules lying on the deep-seabed floor. In part, it was the newfound ability to recover the oil under the continental shelf that spurred the Truman proclamations. The desire to protect coastal waters also grew out of developments in the distant-water fishing industry. Because the yields of American coastal fishermen could be threatened by the Japanese and Russian fishing fleets, and those of South American fishermen by U.S. and other fleets, enclosure was seen as a means to conserve and manage

---

[2]Barry Buzan, *Seabed Politics* (New York: Praeger Publishers, 1976), 8.

this exhaustible resource. Finally, the technological possibility of recovering resources lying on the deep-seabed floor placed a new issue on the international agenda. Primarily in Pacific waters, 13,000- to 16,500-feet deep, lie polymetallic nodules containing commercially valuable concentrations of manganese, nickel, copper, and cobalt.[3] New recovery technology raised the question of resource ownership. For those countries with the potential to bring the nodules to the surface, some form of enclosure would guarantee an environment stable enough to make the necessary investments.

Unilateral claims increased, fueled by technological imperatives and more demands for ocean resources due to growing populations and rising incomes. These demands brought the interests of coastal and distant-water fisherman into conflict and engendered complex management and protection problems. Enclosure was also frequently framed as a means toward satisfying claims of distributive justice. The assertion of exclusive fishing zones in South America, for example, were in part prompted by the perception that the distant-water fleets of the United States were once again taking advantage of the resources of the Third World. The heightened consciousness of the Third World brought an increase in unilateral claims in the attempt to ward off the first world.

There were also political sources for the pressures for enclosure. The dramatic increase in demand for oil and strategic minerals drove nations to protect whatever reserves were found off their coasts. Enclosure thus became cloaked with national security justifications, many of which grew out of nationalist sentiments and internal political promptings. For some states, enclosure was seen as a way to be protected from real or imagined threats.

The issues that came to dominate the law of the sea negotiations developed in a variety of forums. Claims were often unilaterally made, to which other nations often unilaterally responded. For example, through the 1950s and 1960s Latin American countries sometimes attempted to enforce their claims to the fishing rights off their coasts by seizing American fishing boats. The U.S. government responded by compensating American fishermen, pressuring Latin American governments, and appealing to regional forums. An attempt to redress the erosion of the freedom of the seas regime was made on a global scale at the 1958 and 1960 UNCLOS conferences.

In 1958, at the first United Nations Conference on the Law of the Sea, 700 delegates from eighty-six countries came to an agreement over four conventions. The Convention on the Continental Shelf essentially

---

[3]Ibid., xvii.

codified the Truman proclamations. It established the rights of a coastal state over the natural resources of the continental shelf out to 200-meters depth or beyond "to where the depth of the superjacent waters admits of the exploration of the natural resources of said areas." The conference also arrived at a Convention on the Territorial Sea and Contiguous Zone, a Convention on the High Seas, and a Convention on Fisheries. A substantial number of states ratified the conventions establishing resource rights to the continental shelf, 12-mile contiguous zones, and reaffirming the freedom of navigation, fishing, and overflight in the high seas. Fewer nations ratified the convention attempting to balance the interest of coastal and distant-water fishing. However, the work of UNCLOS I was largely incomplete because it failed to establish the breadth of the territorial sea and the related fishing zone, to delineate the limits of the continental shelf, and to consider the issues of the deep seabed. Nevertheless, the work of UNCLOS I was a success compared with the results of UNCLOS II.

The closest UNCLOS II came to accomplishing something meaningful was in setting the width of the territorial sea. However, the conference fell one vote short of establishing a 6-mile territorial sea and a 6-mile fisheries zone. Only two resolutions were passed: one to encourage technical assistance on fishing for developing countries and another to fund and publish the records of the conference.

Overall, these conferences did not successfully deal with the breakdown of the freedom of the seas regime. Maritime states (those states that can be considered sea powers and that have an interest in maintaining high seas freedoms) were generally dissatisfied by the lack of an international agreement on the territorial sea. Guaranteed passage through straits was a primary concern, since increases in the width of the territorial sea could close off international straits and restrict naval mobility. Developing states were dissatisfied by the conferences' failure to recognize a 12-mile territorial zone and a fishing zone. Latin American countries in particular considered both demands as prophylactics against the continued encroachment by the developed countries and as necessary to establish strong, independent economies. Finally, because newly independent African states had not participated in the conferences, questions were raised regarding the legitimacy of the conferences' results.

UNCLOS III not only responded to the perceived erosion of the freedom of the seas regime but also provided a forum for settling the issues of the deep seabed, many of which had already been raised in the UN. In the 1960s scientific evidence had suggested that untold wealth for the taking lay on the ocean floor. In a 1967 speech to the

UN the ambassador of Malta, Arvid Pardo, argued that the resources found on the deep seabed were part of "the common heritage of mankind." What he meant by this phrase was that the manganese nodules lying on the bottom of the ocean were not the property of any single nation. All nations had an equal claim to this resource regardless of a state's capabilities or size. According to Pardo, the task of the next ocean regime could be seen as "a race between 'the good of one' (meaning the nation-state acting in its own selfish interest) and 'the common good' (meaning the United Nations and other international organizations)."[4]

---

[4]Robert A. Goldwin, "Locke and the Law of the Sea," *Commentary* vol. 71, no. 6 (June 1981), 49.

Participants, Power, and Interests

DIVERGENT INTERESTS

Before turning to the UNCLOS III negotiations, it is important to consider how nations were divided over the issues. Because more than 160 nations engaged in the negotiations, the number of factions was enormous. Different interests concerning the traditional issues of maritime law (for example, width of territorial sea, nature of contiguous zone, extent of high seas freedoms), were voiced by territorialists (Latin American nations claiming a 200-mile territorial sea), broad margin states (states that wanted sovereign rights to the continental shelf when it extended beyond 200 miles), patrimonialists (states that desired a 200-mile economic or resource zone), archipelagic states (countries which wanted, among other things, "archipelagic waters" plus a 200 mile resource zone), maritime states (states concerned with preserving as much of the old regime as possible), and landlocked and geographically disadvantaged states (states with no access to the oceans or whose access was to a resource-poor or narrow continental margin).[5]

Extensive divisions also emerged over the nontraditional issue of deep-seabed mining. Those states with the technology to mine wanted to establish a regime that was most conducive to bringing the minerals up to the surface. Those states that exported the minerals wished to establish a regime that would either forestall or impose production limits on seabed mining. These limits would ensure that deep-seabed mining did not prove too competitive with their land-based production. A further faction consisted of states that consumed, or were net importers of, the minerals found in the nodules. Like the technologically advanced states, these countries had an interest in mining the minerals in the most cost-effective way possible. Other states possessed deposits of

---

[5]These divisions are taken from Ann Hollick, *U.S. Foreign Policy and the Law of the Sea* (Princeton, N.J.: Princeton University Press, 1981), 251–55.

these nodules near or in possible contiguous zones. Their interest, assuming the availability of technology, would be similar to that of the land-based producers. Perhaps the most cohesive faction was the "Group of 77" states that brought a set of ideological and economic interests to the conference. The interests of these countries lay in establishing a regime that could control mining, divide revenue, and serve as a precedent for larger New International Economic Order (NIEO) issues. Finally, an eastern bloc faction, interested in mining sometime in the future, primarily wanted to gain favor with the developing states.

From the American perspective the complexity of negotiations, given the range of international factions, was compounded by the extent of domestic divisions within the United States. Significant bureaucratic divisions within the executive branch included the departments of Defense, State, Interior, and Commerce. All of these departments had an interest in how the American negotiating stance was formulated. The primary interest of the Department of Defense was in preserving the mobility of the navy by ensuring high seas freedoms and guaranteeing transit through straits. The State Department wanted the negotiations to ensure good international relations and arrive at a mutually acceptable treaty. Securing oil rights to a broadly defined continental shelf was the Interior Department's hope, while Commerce sought to protect fishing rights and establish access to the deep seabed for U.S. companies.

Congress also sought to influence the negotiations. For example, Senate committees on interior and insular affairs and the subcommittee on the outer continental shelf applied political pressure on different administrations to develop positions favorable to their constituencies. These constituencies included lobbying groups from the oil industry, coastal fishing industry, distant-water fishing industry, and mining industry. All had vested interests in a new regime.

The oil industry advanced the most insistent claims for enclosure. The strength of its efforts to extend state jurisdiction to minerals beneath the entire continental margin was felt primarily during the first stage of the conference. Similarly, coastal fishermen also pressed for greater enclosure to protect fishing stocks off U.S. coasts. In contrast, distant-water fishermen saw the extension of coastal state jurisdiction as a threat to their livelihood. They feared a regime that would legitimize the types of seizures that had beset American fishermen off South American coasts in the 1950s and 1960s. Finally, the hard minerals industry became a powerful influence during the second part of the conference, when deep-seabed mining was discussed. Beginning in the late 1970s, companies that believed in the potential of mining the ocean floor pressed American negotiators to advance the least intrusive international regime possible, a position that resonated most strongly in the Reagan administration.

THE CONFLICT OF AMERICAN INTERESTS

The wide variety of interest groups and factions that had, or attempted to have, influence over the negotiating stance of the United States raises the question of the nature of U.S. interests. Was it in the national interest to attempt to preserve the freedom of the seas regime, or had that regime lost its utility in serving U.S. economic, political, and military goals? Was it true that U.S. postwar interests could best be served by greater enclosure? Did the United States' position as a great naval power necessitate preserving the regime of freedom of the seas? How did U.S. strategic requirements relate to the liberties sanctioned by this regime? How had this regime protected other U.S. political and economic interests with regard to ocean use? Could an alternative regime better serve these interests?

Understanding where U.S. interests lay is no idle exercise, for it is widely understood that "parties generally engage in negotiations with the expectation that their interests will be better served by a joint agreement than by the unilateral alternatives each side would pursue in the case of no-agreement."[6] The fundamental problem for the United States in the law of the sea negotiations was the lack of a consensus over U.S. interests. More properly, the United States possessed a broad set of competing interests, and the U.S. position in the negotiations would depend on which set of interests were judged more valuable.

As a nation with thousands of miles of coastline and valuable fishing and oil resources located above and below a wide continental shelf, the United States is clearly a coastal power: a state whose coastal interests would be served by greater enclosure of ocean space. Indeed, it was these interests that were largely served by the Truman proclamations of 1945. U.S. coastal interests, primarily framed in economic terms, led some to advocate the creation of economic or trusteeship zones, which would grant the United States exclusive economic rights to coastal resources. In contrast, U.S. maritime interests were framed in terms of security—how the oceans could be used to ensure security and meet

---

[6]James K. Sebenius, *Negotiating the Law of the Sea* (Cambridge, MA: Harvard Universtiy Press, 1984), 72.

American commitments abroad. As Robert E. Osgood described them in 1976:

> U.S. military security interests, broadly conceived, lie in the effective use of four zones of ocean space—the seabed, the surface, the subsurface, and the superjacent air—in order to: (1) maintain an adequate strategic nuclear capability; (2) maintain an adequate capacity to project American forces overseas in local wars; (3) protect U.S. citizens, commerce, and access to vital resources in peacetime; (4) maintain adequate intelligence and military surveillance capabilities; and (5) protect the sea-lanes, project forces abroad, maintain combat capabilities and perform other naval functions in a more-than-local war.[7]

The kind of international regime that would advance these interests would, among other things, have to protect unimpeded and submerged passage for nuclear submarines, overflight rights over straits, commercial transport of oil, and the deployment and resupply capabilities of the navy.

Although enclosure was a welcomed development to supporters of U.S. coastal interests, it was seen as a nightmare to those advancing the United States' maritime interests. For the navy, any extension of national sovereignty was a potential threat—either in its direct consequences or as a precedent—to its mission. Defense Department officials repeatedly made the case that if territorial seas were extended only 12 nautical miles, "'Traditional activities in 116 international straits less than 24 miles in width could be restricted."[8] Preserving naval mobility appeared to require that high seas freedom in the straits be protected worldwide. Furthermore, the navy sought to prevent "creeping jurisdiction,"[9] by which high seas freedoms could be eroded in a piecemeal but very steady fashion. The navy viewed any enclosure as a very slippery slope, since claims incrementally extending the jurisdiction

---

[7]Robert E. Osgood, "U.S. Security Interests and the Law of the Sea" in Ryan C. Amacher and Richard James Sweeney, eds., *The Law of the Sea* (Washington, D.C.: American Enterprise Institute for Public Policy Research, 1976), 11.

[8]Sebenius, *Negotiating the Law of the Sea,* 74.

[9]Ann Hollick points out that immediately after World War II, until the late 1960s, "The central problem...arising from the exploration of seabed resources, was not that of creeping jurisdiction. Rather it was the need to provide for the accommodation of multiple uses of the ocean environment." The navy assumed that "freedom of the seas could be maintained under an expanding shelf regime." (Hollick, *U.S. Foreign Policy and the Law of the Sea,* 185). This view apparently changed with the Henkin Report (1967) and the Stratton Commission Report (1969). With these reports, the developments in the law of the sea came to be seen as a "trend" of crisis proportions. The effect of these reports was a redefinition of the problem facing the navy. Instead of accommodating multiple uses of the ocean, the objective was to stop creeping jurisdiction.

of coastal powers could be used as precedent for more expansive claims. Consequently, the Department of Defense favored not only free passage through straits but restrictions on economic claims to offshore areas, a narrow definition of the continental shelf, and an international seabed regime. Whatever deterred further national extensions was seen as good for U.S. maritime interests.

Opinions about how best to balance and pursue U.S. interests shifted with administrations. During the Nixon administration it was felt that the United States, to advance its maritime interests, would have to forgo satisfying its coastal interests. That trade-off was rejected by the Ford administration, and the belief that maritime interests could be satisfied without sacrificing coastal interests continued through the Carter administration. However, the United States still believed that both interests could be guaranteed only through multilateral negotiations. All this was to change with the Reagan administration. Not only did the multilateral negotiation process cease to be considered necessary to secure maritime interests, but many believe that U.S. coastal interests were awarded more significance than were U.S. maritime interests. To see this shift, it is necessary to examine the Nixon administration's initial decision to begin negotiations.

Precipitants and Conditions

For the United States as a coastal power in the late 1960s, the trend in ocean politics could be viewed as both encouraging and perhaps inevitable. The trend toward greater enclosure was seen as encouraging to U.S. coastal interests because it meant that coastal resources could be explored and developed without the interference of other states. The call for larger economic and territorial zones by coastal interests worldwide created the impression that the breakdown of the freedom of the seas regime was inevitable.

Does this breakdown of the freedom of the seas regime and the strength of coastal interests in the United States and abroad explain the Nixon administration's decision to negotiate? More broadly, would these interests be better served by a new regime formalized through treaty or evolved through custom?

A strong argument could be made that, even at the time of the Nixon administration, U.S. coastal interests would have been better served by the no-treaty option. Given the worldwide trend to increase territorial and economic zones, not only would U.S. coastal interests be served by "going it alone," but the practice of "going it alone" would appear to be characteristic of the emerging international regime. Domestic legislation that created and regulated offshore conservation and economic zones could significantly advance these interests. Those groups representing U.S. coastal interests (coastal fishermen, the oil lobby, and the Department of Interior) believed that U.S. economic interests required direct control over oil and a broad definition of the continental margin.

Consequently, during the Nixon administration some of these groups fought hard to stalemate a bureaucratic process that was attempting to advance an international proposal. An alternative approach could be found in seeking to resolve conflicting claims through bilateral, ad hoc solutions as problems arose. A state with the will and capability to enforce and protect its coastal interests may indeed renounce any negotiating forum.

U.S. maritime interests, however, were also at stake and pivoted on the issue of naval mobility. Did this strategic necessity require guaranteed freedom of transit through and above straits? According to Robert E. Osgood, "Even the most restrictive of these regimes [enclosure] would not undermine America's strategic capability on the ocean, particularly if the Trident System were in operation."[10] But in the late 1960s and early 1970s the Trident System was not in operation, and an international regime that closed off many of the most important straits could have posed a threat to U.S. strategic capabilities. Moreover, given the United States' interests and capabilities in the late 1960s and its commitment to a global presence, free passage and overflight rights were essential.

Additional concerns about naval mobility focused on national claims to the continental shelf, economic zones, and the deep seabed. Was it reasonable to resist such creeping jurisdiction on strategic grounds? Claims for 200-mile territorial seas, already made by Argentina, Brazil, Ecuador, El Salvador, Panama, Peru, Sierra Leone, and Uruguay, exacerbated fears of the slippery slope of creeping jurisdiction. If this claim became the norm, the "200-mile territorial zones would completely cover the Mediterranean, the Baltic, the North Sea, the Persian Gulf and the South China Sea."[11] But how likely was it that other states

---

[10]Osgood, "U.S. Security Interests and the Law of the Sea," 24.
[11]Finn Laursen, *Superpower at Sea* (New York: Praeger Publishers, 1983), 35.

would make such expansive claims? How many states actually respected the claims of the territorialists? Did claims to the economic resources on the continental shelf establish a dangerous precedent and threaten U.S. security?

A decision to enter a multilateral negotiating forum, based on the belief that creeping jurisdiction was real and must be prevented to secure naval mobility, would hinge on the assessments of what price the United States would have to pay to achieve its goals. The choice for the Nixon administration was never treaty versus no treaty, but a treaty at a particular cost versus no treaty at a particular cost. Obviously, a treaty that guaranteed high seas freedoms and passage through and above straits, obtained at little cost, would be the best possible solution. But could one expect that the rest of the world would be willing to guarantee the maritime interests of the Great Powers? Alternatively, could U.S. maritime interests be sufficiently advanced on a bilateral, ad hoc basis?

The Department of Defense assessed the price of securing naval mobility to be concessions on the deep-seabed interests of the Third World. Generally, Defense officials found this cost acceptable and favored a treaty that would create an international regime to regulate exploration and exploitation of the deep seabed, a step they believed would inhibit jurisdictional creep. The deep seabed was seen as a bargaining chip that would facilitate a quid pro quo between the maritime powers and the Third World. The Third World would receive certain ideological and economic advantages, and the United States would secure its maritime interests.

The cost for obtaining the same goals without a treaty may have appeared uncertain, at best, to the Nixon administration. By relying on formal and informal agreements as well as on explicit and implicit incentives and threats, the navy's mission could probably be secured but at a greater cost. Given the breakdown of the freedom of seas regime and the lack of worldwide agreement, questions regarding the legitimacy of U.S. navigational and overflight rights could always be raised. In the absence of a consensus over the legitimacy of these rights and given the cost of using force, "going it alone" was not risk free.

The Third World position regarding coastal and maritime rights was even more complex. Third World states generally sought economic protection through large territorial limits and resource zones and thus supported the coastal bloc far more than the maritime bloc. Nevertheless, the Third World was far from monolithic on this issue. Divisions existed between landlocked Third World states (which feared that large resource zones would deprive them of the opportunity to fish) and coastal Third World states, between states that sought to challenge the developed states on navigation rights and states that resisted their view of freedom of navigation, and between states that sought to create a new economic order and those less ideologically motivated.

Should the United States go to the bargaining table? Which interests are more important? Would UNCLOS III necessarily advance those interests? Should the no-treaty option be seriously considered?

For the Nixon administration, the primary objective was to ensure American naval mobility. The administration believed that the most propitious means to secure the necessary freedom through and above straits was by stopping creeping jurisdiction and that the best way to do this was through international agreement. Moreover, administration officials felt that to halt the trend toward enclosure, and establish an outer limit to the continental shelf, it was essential to deal with the seabed issue. Resolving the problem of creeping jurisdiction required a link between the issues of naval mobility and the deep seabed. It should be noted that this linkage did not direct a particular type of international regime over the seabed—only that the issue be settled in a way that claims to mineral resources could not disrupt the freedoms on the superjacent water.

Process
Prenegotiations

The Nixon administration's decision to submit a proposal to the UN Seabed Committee in August 1970 entailed not only an understanding of the nature of U.S. interests but an understanding of what the general form of the treaty should be. The decision was whether to negotiate a comprehensive treaty or break the issues down into manageable packages. Through the 1960s both the United States and the Soviet Union tried to keep the seabed issue apart from the other issues. As late as 1969 the superpowers voted against a General Assembly Resolution calling for a law of the sea conference.

What are the advantages and disadvantages of negotiating a comprehensive treaty as opposed to a series of treaties on different issue areas? Which approach is most advantageous to the various participants?

In pragmatic terms, the point of manageable packages is just that: to make things more manageable. Given the tremendous scope of the issues and the staggering number of participants, the attempt to arrive at a comprehensive law of the sea treaty appeared daunting. Also, manageable packages could alleviate the problem of time-consuming coalition building. In tactical terms, throwing everything into the hopper would mean that each issue would not be negotiated on its merits. Under a comprehensive treaty, linkages would inevitably be created, and agreement would be only the result of the lowest common denominator.

There were, however, reasons for not breaking the negotiations down into manageable packages. The simple physical connection between the seabed and the superjacent water "lent intellectual and political plausibility to a bargaining linkage."[12] Moreover, many nations viewed the possible linkages between the various issue areas as advantageous. For example, the Third World expected concessions on seabed questions in return for satisfying the interests of the maritime powers.[13] Broadening the range of topics, they felt, would increase their leverage in negotiations.

The Nixon administration eventually submitted a proposal to the United Nations calling for the renunciation of national claims to seas beyond the depth of 200 meters, the creation of a trusteeship zone in which the coastal state would have access to resources at the continental margin, the development of international machinery to "authorize and regulate exploration and use of seabed resources,"[14] and a 12-mile limit for territorial seas on the condition that free transit through international straits was guaranteed. The Nixon proposal implied that the United States was willing not only to negotiate a law of the sea treaty but to negotiate a comprehensive treaty. The proposal's immediate effect was to infuse new life into the United Nation's efforts to negotiate a new international regime. But the proposal also unleashed a wave of domestic opposition and resistance, giving birth to new interest groups that would become significant as negotiations proceeded.

Once the decision was made to negotiate a comprehensive law of the sea treaty, three committees were established to deal with the issues. Committee I was primarily concerned with issues surrounding the use of the deep seabed. Committee II was charged with drawing up that part of the treaty dealing with, and defining the traditional subjects of, maritime law and was to establish the rights and responsibilities

---

[12]Sebenius, *Negotiating the Law of the Sea,* 76.
[13]Ibid.
[14]Laursen, *Superpower at Sea,* 6.

regarding the territorial sea, international straits, the contiguous zone, the continental shelf, fishing and the high seas. Committee III was responsible for regulations regarding scientific aspects of the ocean: pollution, scientific research, and the transfer of marine technology.

The negotiations themselves were to proceed on the basis of consensus, and voting was to serve only as a final resort. The UNCLOS III procedural rules set out the rationale for consensus:

> Bearing in mind that the problems of ocean space are closely related and need to be examined as a whole and the desirability of adopting a convention on the Law of the Sea which will ensure the widest possible acceptance, the Conference should make every effort to reach an agreement on substantive matters by way of consensus and there should be no voting on such matters until all efforts at consensus have been exhausted.[15]

To facilitate this consensus, committee chairmen were given wide latitude to modify the texts based on how talks were proceeding. The power of committee chairmen combined with the consensus rule gave the participants greater maneuvering room to develop ideas, linkages, and agreements that would have been stifled by the public and more official mechanisms of voting. The primary disadvantage to moving by consensus is that it is a slow and tedious process. Although giving greater power to committee chairmen mitigates this difficulty, it creates potential problems of its own, for such power is subject to abuse.

---

[15]Clyde Sanger, *Ordering the Oceans* (Toronto: University of Toronto Press, 1987), 37–38.

Process
Formula

The first years of formal negotiation signaled that the United States had abandoned its formula of trading coastal rights for maritime rights. In part, resistance by coastal rights advocates both in the United States and from other countries caused the U.S. position to shift. The United States conditionally accepted the idea of a 200-mile economic zone in 1974, and in 1976 it dramatically extended its jurisdiction over fishing rights. Although freedom of navigation was preserved in this economic zone, the United States had clearly backtracked from its maritime emphasis. The end of the Vietnam War and concern about getting embroiled in other Third World conflicts weakened the navy's argument that it needed to maintain global commitments. Equally important, the Arab oil boycott of 1973 increased the importance of the United States' developing coastal oil reserves; enclosure, in some ways, no longer seemed to be such a bad idea.

The American retreat from a strong maritime position at first seemed to open the way for a broader agreement. The United Kingdom and the Soviet Union also accepted the 200-mile economic zone. Although the landlocked states were obviously unhappy, the Third World considered this shift by the maritime powers to be a victory. However, the United States had not abandoned, but only modified, its maritime position. Agreement was stalled because: (1) nations located on straits sought to regulate closely the types of ships they would allow to pass; (2) landlocked and geographically disadvantaged states continued to demand access to the sea and its economic resources; (3) the precise character of the economic zone (was it to be governed by the conventions of the high seas, territorial seas, or was it to bear a unique set of rights and obligations), the rights with regard to the territorial sea, and the extent and definition of the continental shelf (some of which extended beyond the 200-mile economic zone) had yet to be established.

Virtually all of these issues were resolved in favor of the United States. This success was partially due to specific tactics the United States adopted in Committee II negotiations. Recognizing that the Third

World was not a monolithic bloc, the United States (as well as other countries) worked with different groups of states to achieve acceptable compromises. For example, the United States obtained concessions on the straits, regarding transit passage and overflight, by dividing the coastal-straits from the archipelagic-straits states. The United States made concessions to Fiji, Indonesia, Malaysia, Mauritius, and the Philippines in exchange for their support of U.S. claims for free passage through and above coastal straits. "The final archipelago articles (Pt. 11, Arts. 117–130) were extremely generous to the archipelagic group. Archipelagic states were allowed to draw straight baselines linking the outermost points of their outermost islands and drying reefs to enclose archipelagic waters."[16] This linkage isolated the coastal-straits states. The U.S. position was strengthened by the time of the Geneva session in 1975 because developing countries had begun to view the demands of the coastal-straits states with increasing suspicion as they came to understand their own dependence on the straits for oil export and import.

Committee II also resolved problems concerning the continental shelf by providing for international revenue sharing between the area where the 200-mile economic zone ended and where the shelf ended. Other agreements called for limiting territorial water to 12 miles, extending resource rights for coastal states to 200 miles, assuring freedom of navigation, and establishing the right to sue a state that interfered with any of these rights. Each point represented significant benefits to both the maritime and coastal interests of the United States.

American successes in Committee II can be attributed not only to a softening of the U.S. maritime position and the exploitation of particular cleavages but also to a pliancy in the Third World's position. The willingness of the Third World to accept many of these maritime freedoms stemmed from a perception that the negotiations of Committee II could ultimately be linked to Committee I negotiations. In other words, they believed that cooperation with the developed states on maritime matters could result in a regime favorable to their own deep-seabed interests.

Committee III, charged with regulating scientific research, also confronted conflicting maritime and coastal interests. Maritime states generally resisted, while coastal states demanded, greater environmental control and regulation. Given its coastal interests, the United States sided with the environmentalists, but because of its maritime interests it ultimately argued for minimal powers of enforcement for coastal

---

[16]Hollick, *U.S. Foreign Policy and the Law of the Sea*, 305.

states. Among the developed states, Canada pushed hardest for the development of international environmental law.

Differing positions on the environment, however, did not create a clean maritime/coastal split among nations. Some developing coastal states (for example, India, Indonesia, and Kenya) strongly favored greater power to the coastal state. Other developing coastal states believed that economic development should take priority over environmental concerns and pressed for special status in the application of environmental regulations. The desire for unimpeded economic development and navigation, on the one hand, and for greater coastal control, on the other, eventually split the Group of 77.

Nevertheless, negotiators continually attempted to balance the enforcement and regulatory powers of the coastal states against the navigational concerns of the maritime states. Under the freedom of the seas regime, maritime interests had been advantaged: only the flag state (the state in which a ship was registered) was authorized to enforce pollution controls. By 1979 a formula more favorable to the coastal states was developed. Under the treaty, the flag state retained responsibility for punishing violators, but the coastal states could inspect, initiate proceedings against, and detain ships that had transgressed environmental standards. The standards, however, had to be internationally acceptable so as to avoid unduly burdening navigation. Consequently, they did not apply to any warship, vessel, or aircraft used for governmental, noncommercial service. Thus, overall, the maritime states were successful in fending off an environmental regime that accorded significant power to the coastal states.

In dealing with the issue of how states should conduct scientific research in the exclusive economic zones (EEZs), Committee III was split between the developed and developing states. The central goal of the developed states was to secure the right to conduct research in the EEZs with as few regulations as possible. Developing coastal states wanted to precondition all research to the consent of the coastal states. Their reasoning, according to Canadian lawyer Leonard Legault, was that the current regime of research freedom had not benefited the Third World:

> Because they understand the economic uses of marine scientific research, they view freedom of research as a pathway for the erosion of their sovereign rights over the resources of the economic zone.... Perhaps they forget that you do not gain freedom in one field by denying it in another. But I am sure they are right in saying that "pure" research is a rare thing: Einstein and a bit of chalk—but that led to the atomic bomb. Knowledge is power, they say: and who can

disagree? How, they ask, can they manage their resources if those wishing to exploit them know more about them than they do? How can they bring about a real transfer of technology if they cannot participate meaningfully in all research within their economic zone? And how can they truly participate without control?[17]

Even given their differences, all parties agreed that consent to do research within the territorial sea must be obtained from the coastal state. The problem was how to deal with research in the EEZs. Essentially four positions emerged: a large group of developing coastal states argued for the right to control completely all marine research in the economic zone. The second group consisted of states (for example, Australia, Canada, Ireland, and Mexico) that essentially agreed with the developing coastal states but argued that research should not be placed under unreasonable restrictions. The third negotiating position (held, for example, by Denmark, East Germany, Poland, the Soviet Union, and the United Kingdom) argued that consent should be a prerequisite only when the research related to the exploitation of minerals. This position, of course, would permit research related to military considerations. The fourth position, held by the United States and some West European states, held out for the least intrusive regime possible— one that would guarantee the widest sphere of research freedom.

A compromise was proposed that divided research into two types. Research associated with resource development would require consent, while research unrelated to resource development could be conducted without obtaining permission from the relevant coastal state. In the formula that eventually developed, the distinction between applied and fundamental research was ultimately rejected as unworkable, enhancing the authority of the developing coastal states. Under the treaty, research could be conducted within an EEZ only with the explicit or tacit consent of the relevant states. To obtain such consent, researchers would be required to explain the project, give the host state a right to participate, and agree to make their findings known to the host. If the host state did not reply to the proposal within four months, researchers could assume that the coastal state tacitly consented to the project.

Perhaps the most difficult negotiations were those of Committee I concerning how best to mine minerals beyond the 200-mile limit. Both economic and ideological issues divided the developed states (led by the United States) and the Third World on this issue. Economic questions centered on the most appropriate regime for mining minerals in international waters. Because of the level of technology, investment,

---

[17]Sanger, *Ordering the Oceans*, 128.

and risk involved, only a few developed countries could mine the seabed. An international regime needed to be established that would provide incentives for the developed states (and private companies) to mine the seabed but that would also guarantee access by Third World countries. Ideological questions concerned ownership of the seabed minerals. Did they, as the Third World maintained, belong to everyone or, as the United States asserted, to no one? What did the phrase "the common heritage of mankind" truly mean?

The United States wanted unencumbered access to the minerals on the ocean floor—in particular, the strategic minerals of manganese and cobalt, which are found in great abundance on the seabed and which are necessary for steel production. The fact that the United States imports virtually all of its manganese and cobalt from a few land-based sources, and the possibility that the Soviet Union and South Africa could be the major producers of manganese by the turn of the century, meant that future access to supplies could not be guaranteed. Given this dependence, the United States wanted any law of the sea treaty to ensure the availability of the seabed. Beginning with the August 1970 draft treaty, the United States agreed to the creation of an international authority that would license mining by both private companies and states. The very existence of such an authority was a concession by the United States, because it presented at least a potential obstacle to private companies' developing the seabed. To guard against undue international control that could stifle private mining, the United States insisted that the industrially advanced states be granted greater powers, including the right to veto the authority's decisions. Only with this control, American negotiators argued, would private companies feel they could justify the costs and risks associated with deepseabed mining.

Third World nations disagreed. They countered that if the seas were truly "the common heritage of mankind," a powerful international authority would be needed to represent all nations equally. The seabed authority would be reduced to merely a means guaranteeing the access of developed states if voting was weighted in their favor. In contrast, the Third World states advocated an authority (subsequently labeled the Enterprise) with supranational powers, including the ability to exploit the nodules and distribute the revenues. Power within the Enterprise would be equally distributed, reflecting the fact that the seabed belonged to all. Arvid Pardo wrote:

> The oceans involve the interests of all, and all must therefore work together to establish an equitable regime beneficial to all. Present

law of the sea based on freedom and sovereignty is being rapidly
eroded by technology and events and is, in any case, incapable of
providing a lasting framework for the beneficial use of ocean space
under present conditions. A new basis for a new regime must be
created.[18]

The issue of ownership of seabed minerals exacerbated the dispute
between the Third World and the developed states, with Third World
delegates arguing that the nodules lying on the ocean floor were not
within any nation's jurisdiction and thus belonged to all mankind. Because everyone owned the minerals, they continued, only an international authority committed to distributing equitably the revenues from
mining should be allowed to operate. An individual state or private mining company recovering the nodules would, in effect, be stealing them
from their rightful owners—the rest of the world. At the very least,
the international authority should control who mined, how much they
mined, and how the revenues were distributed. At the most, such an
authority would undertake the mining itself.

Third World states also pointed out that a strong international
authority had certain political advantages, because it would be heavi-
ly supported by the developing, landlocked, and geographically disadvantaged states. If successful, such a formula could also provide a stable environment for mining and begin to meet the developing states'
claims to distributive justice. Finally, a strong seabed authority would
provide a precedent for peacefully and cooperatively dealing with common areas and resources in the future.

The practical difficulties of enacting this formula were enormous.
If the authority itself was to engage in mining, how would it obtain
the means to do so from the few developed states that had the technology and capital? Without the proper incentives, developed states
might be reluctant to participate and could foreclose the authority's
success. The United States in particular was reluctant to agree to such
a formula because of the distribution of authority in the Enterprise's
voting arrangements. Opponents of the treaty in the United States
feared that establishing a strong international authority would serve
as an unfortunate precedent. Northcutt Ely wrote:

> Once the principle is conceded that an agency of the United Nations
> shall have the inherent power to deny, grant, condition and revoke
> a nation's power to use the bed of the sea for production of minerals,
> it becomes difficult to say why, on principle, the international authority

[18]Arvid Pardo, "New Institutions for Ocean Space," in Elisabeth Mann Borgese and David
Krieger, eds., *The Tides of Change* (New York: Mason Charter, 1975), 325.

should not have similar competence to grant or deny use of the seabed for all purposes, including peaceful military uses, and, indeed, to grant or deny use of the water column itself.[19]

The developed states argued that the nodules were not owned by everyone but by no one; because no one owned the nodules, they were available to anyone who could take them. To legitimize their position, they drew on John Locke's argument that the acquisition of private property in a "state of nature" is created by labor. If the Third World countries lacked the resources to develop the nodules, they could not own them. In other words, the seabed was *res nullius*, it belonged to no one and therefore was open to claim by anyone who worked for it.

> When the assertion is made that the deep seas are the common heritage of mankind, it does not mean that every human being is a part owner of the international waters; much less can it mean that every nation considered sovereign is somehow part owner. What it means is that international waters are unowned. Thus when something must be done to make sensible rules for the use of these waters and the resources in them, nations come to the conference table in the status of non-owners.[20]

There were a number of formulas that could reflect the unowned character of the seabed. The least intrusive regime would be one in which companies and states simply mined where they wanted. Under this regime, it would be the miners' responsibility to protect their claims. A somewhat more intrusive, but still acceptable, regime would allow mining either under the auspices of a flag state or under a larger regional regime in which like-minded states guaranteed each other's claims (a formula eventually advocated under the name of the mini-treaty solution). In 1970 the United States suggested perhaps the most intrusive international regime, which remained true to the spirit of the seabed as *res nullius*. Under this system, mining would be left to the initiative of the individual state or corporation. The miner would stake a claim, register it with the international authority, and expect that this claim would be respected by others.

According to the developed states, the advantages of these kinds of "hands-off" formulas were numerous: There would be no incentive to create a bloated, inefficient, international bureaucracy to establish

[19]Northcutt Ely, "United States Seabed Minerals Policy," *Natural Resources Lawyer* 4 (July 1971): 614–15.
[20]Goldwin, "Locke and the Law of the Sea," 48.

production limits and prices. Nor would such regimes require massive capital and technology transfers. The market would decide when, where, and how much to mine. If mining became economically feasible, those states with the capability to mine would mine. Because of these efficiencies, the world would benefit from the increased availability of these minerals, which, under a more intrusive and cumbersome regime would remain, they argued, on the bottom of the ocean.

The disadvantage of the laissez-faire approaches was that they could not muster the support of many nations. Nor would they address many of the Third World's grievances. More important, the demand for a weak seabed authority could put other treaty goals of the developed maritime powers at risk because the Third World had linked gains in Committee I negotiations to concessions in Committee II negotiations. The refusal to create a strong seabed authority could jeopardize the protection of maritime freedoms. (The Third World wanted to convince the first world that "navigation" could be only secured with "nodules.") Furthermore, if a laissez-faire regime generated little international support, mining operations could be threatened. Without a stable international regime that held mining claims to the deep seabed as legitimate, companies could be unwilling to risk the millions of dollars necessary to proceed with mining.

In spite of these risks, the United States envisioned an authority that could not exact payments from companies, license mining firms, require technology transfers, or set prices and production levels but that would have the minimum power to legitimize claims. In short, the United States conceived of a regime in which it possessed sufficient influence to guarantee its interests. The Third World clung to the opposing view on each of these issues, and a stalemate ensued.

What bargaining position should the United States take to protect its interests? Does one conception of property make more sense than the other, and does "sense" depend on the nature of the state? What is the just thing to do? Is the issue a matter of justice at all, or should purely prudential calculations dictate the U.S. position? If prudential calculations are indicated, what kind of policy do they dictate? What formula has the best chance of fostering a consensus between states? What U.S. positions would have the best chance and an acceptable chance of approval by Congress and the various possible interest groups at home? Should the United States accept the linkage between nodules and navigational freedoms?

In 1976 Secretary of State Henry Kissinger offered a number of compromises, which became known as the parallel system. From the American perspective these compromises were quite extensive. The largest concession accorded the Enterprise a right to mine, alongside of companies' and states' rights to mine. The United States did not believe that the Enterprise should exclusively hold this right; private companies and individual states should also be allowed access to seabed minerals. Hence the parallel nature of the formula. Kissinger's formula also offered a system for choosing and developing the parallel mines, known as banking sites; the suggestion of transferring technology and production controls; an agreement to finance the authority; and the safety valve of periodic review. What remained at issue was political control of the authority and the details of the financial and production arrangements.

Although the American position had softened, the developing states of the Group of 77 felt the Kissinger formula demanded even greater concessions on their part. The parallel system itself, by guaranteeing access to companies and individual states, was seen as a violation of "the common heritage of mankind" principle. In response, the Kissinger proposal was subsequently and single-handedly revised by Committee Chairman Paul Engo from Cameroon. These revisions, involving issues of technology transfer, financial liability of contractors, production limitations, voting power, and regulation of scientific research mollified the Group of 77 but upset the United States and led U.S. Ambassador Elliot Richardson to call for a review of the substance and procedure of the conferences. After further negotiations, which reduced the power of committee chairmen to revise the text, the essence of a bargain had emerged in which the United States (and other developed states) would make concessions on the mining issues in exchange for Third World concessions on freedom of navigation.

Process
Closure

The formula of the parallel system allowed negotiators to work rapidly toward closure during the 1979 and 1980 treaty sessions. Although negotiations continued to be difficult, the pace of agreement and compromise accelerated. On the vexing issue of technology transfer, for example, the treaty was altered to oblige the transfer of technology to the Enterprise only if the technology was unavailable on the market, while sections requiring the transfer of technology to developing countries remained. On the critical issue of voting procedures, the parties agreed that different issues would require different majorities. Procedural issues would be decided simply by majority vote, while more substantive issues would require greater majorities or a consensus. Other compromises resulted in agreement or near agreement on scientific research and production controls.

By the fall of 1980 a draft text of the treaty had been endorsed by Elliot Richardson and most other representatives. The treaty contained much that the United States sought—in particular, agreements that codified the doctrine of freedom of the high seas. Even in creating a 200-mile economic zone, the treaty preserved high seas freedoms. Aside from the 200-mile economic zone, the treaty established a 12-mile territorial sea, a 24-mile contiguous zone, and a continental shelf boundary that extended at least 200 miles from the shore baseline. By creating two legal rights of passage the treaty also attempted to allay the concerns of maritime states whose military and commercial interests were threatened by the extension of the territorial sea. In archipelagic waters, states were guaranteed essentially the same right of innocent passage allowed in territorial waters. In passage through straits, freedom of navigation and overflight was guaranteed for continuous and expeditious transit. In both cases the relevant states, along with international organizations, could propose sea-lane and traffic regulations.

The regime established to govern the seabed was based largely on the idea of the parallel system. The treaty described an International

Seabed Authority to include an assembly, council, and the Enterprise. All parties to the treaty would also be members of the assembly. Each state would have one vote in setting general policy, electing members of the council, establishing the Enterprise Governing Board, and distributing the financial benefits of exploiting the seabed. As mentioned earlier, depending on the nature of the issue at hand, different decisions would require different majorities.

The council would be composed of thirty-six members; large investors, major consumers, large land-based exporters of minerals, and other special-interest categories would receive greater representation. Remaining members were to be chosen on the basis of geographic location. The council's purpose was to establish rules for governing the seabed system, to adopt recommendations from an Economic Planning Commission and a Legal and Technical Commission, to select applicants for mining licenses, and to arrange the funding for the authority and the Enterprise. The actual mining, transportation, processing, and marketing of minerals recovered from the seabed devolved to the Enterprise. A fifteen-member governing board and director general would control the Enterprise, and ensuing profits would be treated as "the common heritage of mankind."

Briefly, the parallel system would follow this framework:

- A state, company, consortium, or the Enterprise applies to exploit a worthwhile tract of the seabed. (All private miners must be sponsored by a state that has ratified the treaty. Every seabed tract to be mined must be large enough to support two mining operations.)

- Once the Council approves the application, half the tract is given to the applicant, who now has an exclusive right to mine the area (subject to production limitations on particular minerals). Half the tract is designated a reserved site, which can now be mined by the Enterprise if it develops plans that are technologically and financially sound.

- If the Enterprise decides not to mine the site, other states or private actors can apply to exploit the tract.

Proponents of the treaty argued that the convention assured access to miners, guaranteed a fair return given the risks involved, and protected against the arbitrary power of the authority. Equally important, the treaty promised to improve relations between the United States and the Third World. Although the treaty contained provisions the United States did not like, especially concerning the mining of the seabed, Richardson and others argued that these concessions, embodied in Kissinger's formula of the parallel system, were trivial compared with the gains the treaty would bring about and that the concessions were necessary to "buy" other states' acceptance of points in the treaty that were important to the United States.

At this point, the newly elected Reagan administration transformed the closure phase of negotiations in an attempt to work out a new formula. On March 2, 1981, the administration decided to conduct a policy review of the law of the sea negotiations. The review was concluded and made public on January 29, 1982. Although the administration found much of the treaty acceptable, particularly the sections on freedom of navigation and coastal rights, it rejected the provision on deep-seabed mining. The existing provisions would deter the development of the seabed, officials argued, and would give too much power to the Third World, require U.S. technology transfer, and set a bad precedent by giving an international agency so much authority. The administration proposed that the Enterprise, in essence, be transformed into a claims registry, that the United States have much greater voting power, and that the treaty rid itself of its "offensive" (socialist) ideological nature.

The Group of 77 rejected the Reagan proposals, arguing that they were a direct repudiation of the parallel system and gave full power to private companies and states at the expense of the Enterprise. Once again, the Third World asserted, the principle of "the common heritage of mankind" had been subverted. To bridge the gap, "Good Samaritan" countries proposed several changes that increased U.S. influence in the authority and weakened the provisions for technology transfer. Many of these proposals, over the objections of some developing countries, were then incorporated into the treaty.

Despite the compromises, the Reagan administration remained dissatisfied. Voting power in the authority, for example, would not reflect the financial support that the West would contribute. Moreover, the United States was not assured a seat in the executive council, which would be responsible for implementing the authority's day-to-day decisions. Although the final negotiating sessions had guaranteed representation to the largest consumer of deep-seabed minerals, Washington feared that the Soviet Union could qualify for such a position, depending on how "largest consumer" was defined. The administration argued that the convention did not assure the United States the kind of control over decisionmaking consummate with its financial contribution or interests.

The United States further contended that the establishment of production limitations to protect land-based producers and the authority's ability to tax private production were unreasonable restrictions on its ability to access and develop the strategic minerals lying on the deep seabed. The administration also argued that the idea of creating banking sites and guaranteeing access and technology to the Enterprise provided an unfair competitive advantage over private operations. For example, a private company would be unable to rely on defense-related technology that was nontransferable under U.S. law. Consequently, nontransferable technology that was integral to a private mining operation would have to be either made available (contrary to U.S. law) or not used in production (handicapping the operation).[21] Moreover, U.S. officials argued, because the specific arrangements and ideological nature of the International Seabed Authority would deter economic development, the authority would ultimately threaten U.S. economic and strategic interests and serve as a precedent for a new "global collectivism." The administration came to believe that any seabed regime exceeding the power of a claims registry—but which it could not adequately control—would be too powerful, too extensive, and too vulnerable to hostile interests.

Are the gains won in Committee II negotiations more important than the perceived costs of Committee I's proposals? Are there other considerations of value that would be enhanced by signing the treaty? What are the possible results if the United States does not sign the treaty? Are the unilateral alternatives better than a flawed treaty? How significant are the ideological and philosophical aspects in the decision of whether to sign?

---

[21]James L. Malone, "Who Needs the Sea Treaty?" *Foreign Policy*, no. 54 (Spring 1984): 55.

On April 30, 1982, the United States voted against the final treaty adopted by the third United Nations Conference on the Law of the Sea. The vast majority of the Third World states voted in favor of the treaty, with the USSR and some Western countries abstaining. The United States was the only industrialized nation to vote no. In the final analysis the refusal to sign the treaty was a tangible demonstration of the Reagan administration's displeasure with any developments that would impede the United States' ability to act independently. Most important, the administration concluded that it need not exchange "navigation" for "nodules" but that it could have both: By relying on customary law (and the power of the U.S. military), freedom of navigation could be maintained. By concluding mini-treaties with the handful of other states capable of deep-sea mining and through domestic legislation, the United States could proceed to develop the seabed without the difficulties of working with the authority. The administration rejected the strong international regime and interdependent world that UNCLOS III fostered, considering it an unfavorable precedent and a threat to America's freedom of action. (It should be noted, however, that the notion of an unfavorable precedent was not indisputable. For example, Arvid Pardo argued that the treaty, in fact, was a victory for traditional state interests because it now placed 40 percent of ocean space under some form of national control. This 40 percent was significant because of the hydrocarbons, commercially exploitable minerals, and living resources that it contained.) James L. Malone, President Reagan's special representative, wrote:

> Let me state very emphatically that the United States cannot and will not sign the United Nations Convention on the Law of the Sea. The treaty is fatally flawed and cannot be cured. In its present form it presents a serious threat to U.S. vital national interests and, in fact, to global security. Once more, it is inimical to the fundamental principles of political liberty, private property, and free enterprise. The administration firmly believes that those very principles are the key to economic well-being for all countries—developing as well as developed.[22]

The unilateral course set out by the Reagan administration was not without its own risks and problems. It was unclear whether the mini-treaty option could offer a secure enough environment for deep-seabed mining. The convention required signatory parties to recognize that the only legitimate regime was the one established by the convention. If the treaty was widely recognized, the U.S. government might have to subsidize mining companies for the political risks of being outside the treaty. It was even possible that to engage effectively in mining,

---

[22]Malone, "Who Needs the Sea Treaty?" 63.

American consortia would have to operate out of signatory countries. By being outside the convention, the United States could poison the well for mining even within the treaty. Because the United States would probably be the largest participant in mining, its unilateral action could make deep-seabed mining too risky both inside and outside the convention.

A second problem was inherent in the belief that the United States could rely on customary law to secure its interests. The argument that the treaty simply codified existing international law ran up against the postwar trend of the increasing territorial claims by coastal, straits, and archipelagic states. Indeed, the impetus for an international conference was, in part, the perceived breakdown of customary international law—an uncertainty over exactly what the law prescribed. Furthermore, passage through straits would become dependent on the quality of America's bilateral relations with straits states. If relations with those states soured, the legitimacy of U.S. claims could be diminished by the fact that the treaty made transit right no longer "discretionary, tradable, and disputable." A state that had signed the treaty could always choose to regard it as a package deal, one in which states could not simply pick and choose various articles to follow according to their liking. As Leigh S. Ratiner wrote:

> Moreover, if the United States stays out of the sea law treaty while most nations join it, we risk conflict over American assertions that we are entitled, without participating in the treaty, to rights embodied in it related to navigational freedoms, exclusive economic zones, and jurisdiction over our continental shelf, fisheries, pollution control, and the conduct of marine scientific research.[23]

Proponents for signature argued that by staying out of the treaty the United States reduced the number of options available to it when its "rights" become threatened. The notion that the threat or use of force would always, in the end, guarantee U.S. transit rights ignored the possibility that challenges of these rights need not be blatantly provocative. These rights could be eroded by demands for notification, permission, or delay, and challenges could be based on environmental, safety, or resource grounds. The military option simply might not be a proportional or effective response. In addition, the use of force could become prohibitively expensive if transit rights were effectively challenged throughout the world.

---

[23]Leigh S. Ratiner, "The Costs of American Rigidity," in Bernard H. Oxman, David D. Caron, and Charles L.O. Buderi, eds., *Law of Sea: U.S. Policy Dilemma* (San Francisco, Calif.: ICS Press, 1983), 28.

Postscript

I n order for the treaty to go into effect, sixty nations must ratify the convention. As of the summer of 1989 some forty countries had ratified the treaty, and it is unclear whether the necessary number will be reached in the near future. However, countries have generally abided by those parts of the treaty that strengthened and extended the jurisdiction of states. The promise of enormous wealth on the ocean floor has yet to be fulfilled. Problems with research, development, and production have forced nations and companies to reassess the profitability of engaging in deep-sea mining. To date, large-scale undersea mining operations have not proved economically feasible. Thus, ironically, the issue that stalled and eventually defeated the treaty has yet to become a practical problem. Clearly, the absence of a universal law of the sea treaty has not led to the breakdown of all global norms and understandings regarding the use of the sea. However, the existence and character of those norms and understandings now depend on the less precise instrument of customary international law. To the extent that states unambiguously follow the convention, customary international law has taken the place of ratification. However, it remains debatable whether nonparticipating states can draw on the rights and protections of the convention that, through codification, have changed customary law or are manifested in international practice.

The primary reason that many nations (particularly the United States) came to the bargaining table in the 1970s was that they feared creeping jurisdiction. It has not been demonstrated that the present arrangements can adequately withstand the continuing pressures of enclosure. As long as there is an incentive, coastal states will desire to increase their control over larger portions of the ocean. As long as naval and maritime capabilities retain their military and economic utility, maritime states will strive to stave off regulation and control. UNCLOS III offered the hope that these interests could be accommodated in an orderly and predictable fashion. Without a universal law of the sea treaty, a higher degree of uncertainty exists that the interests of coastal and maritime states can be peacefully and reasonably guaranteed in the future. Yet the Reagan administration may have been correct that U.S. interests can be met without having to make the ideological concessions and establishing the unwanted precedents demanded by the treaty. In the final analysis, only time will tell whether the United States' decision not to sign the treaty was a correct one.

Foreign Policy Institute Publications
Distributed by University Press of America,® Inc.

BOOKS ON INTERNATIONAL AFFAIRS

After Reagan: False Starts, Missed Opportunities and New Beginnings, Simon Serfaty (1988)

Free Trade, Fair Trade? The Reagan Record, Charles Pearson (1988)

Making Defense Reform Work: A Report of the Joint Project on Monitoring Defense Reorganization, Harold Brown and James Schlesinger (1989)

Toward Consensus in Foreign and Defense Policy, Harold Brown, ed. (1989)

Technology and the Limitation of International Conflict, Barry M. Blechman, ed. (1989)

The Future of U.S.-Soviet Relations: Twenty American Initiatives for a New Agenda, Simon Serfaty, ed. (1989)

The Politics of Terrorism: Terror as a State and Revolutionary Strategy, Barry Rubin, ed. (1989)

FPI CASE STUDIES OF DIPLOMATIC NEGOTIATIONS

1. *The Panama Canal Negotiations,* Wm. Mark Habeeb and I. William Zartman (1986)
2. *The New GATT Trade Round,* Charles Pearson and Nils Johnson (1986)
3. *The U.S.-Soviet Conventional Arms Transfer Negotiations,* Barry M. Blechman and Janne E. Nolan (1987)
4. *The 1982 Mexican Debt Negotiations: Response to a Financial Crisis,* Roger S. Leeds and Gale Thompson (1987)
5. *Negotiations on the French Withdrawal from NATO,* Michael M. Harrison and Mark G. McDonough (1987)
6. *SALT I: The Limitations of Arms Negotiations,* Jonathan Haslam and Theresa Osborne (1987)
7. *The May 1983 Agreement Over Lebanon,* Barry Rubin and Laura Blum (1987)
8. *U.S.-Canadian Softwood Lumber: Trade Dispute Negotiations,* Charles F. Doran and Timothy J. Naftali (1987)
9. *Contadora: The Limits of Negotiation,* Bruce Michael Bagley and Juan Gabriel Tokatlian (1987)
10. *The Algerian Gas Negotiations,* I. William Zartman and Antonella Bassani (1987)
11. *The 1972 Simla Agreement: An Asymmetrical Negotiation,* Imtiaz H. Bokhari and Thomas Perry Thornton (1988)
12. *Dialogue and Armed Conflict: Negotiating the Civil War in El Salvador,* Riordan Roett and Frank Smyth (1988)
13. *The U.S.-Brazilian Informatics Dispute,* Ellene A. Felder and Andrew Hurrell (1988)
14. *The United States and the Law of the Sea Treaty,* Steven R. David and Peter Digeser (1989)

FPI POLICY BRIEFS

U.S.-Soviet Trade Policy, Carol Rae Hansen, July 1988

The Allure of Summits, Charles H. Fairbanks, Jr., May 1988

Egypt and U.S. Interests, Alfred Leroy Atherton, Jr., March 1988

Balancing Act: The Republic of Korea Approaches 1988, Ralph N. Clough, September 1987

The United States and the Philippine Bases, Evelyn Colbert, August 1987

Iran's Future: Crises, Contingencies, and Continuities, Barry Rubin, July 1987

Pakistan: Internal Developments and the U.S. Interest, Thomas Perry Thornton, March 1987

Arms Control: A Skeptical Appraisal and a Modest Proposal, Robert E. Osgood, April 1986

Thinking About SDI, Stephen J. Hadley, March 1986

FPI POLICY STUDY GROUPS

The U.S. Approach to the Latin American Debt Crisis, Michael T. Clark et al. (1988)

U.S. Policy Toward the Bretton Woods Institutions, Alvin Paul Drischler and M.P. Benjenk, eds. (1988)

U.S.-Soviet Relations, Simon Serfaty, ed. (1985)

To order copies of these publications, contact Customer Service Department, University Press of America,® Inc., 4720 Boston Way, Lanham, Md. 20706/(301) 459-3366.

Orders for Case Study Teaching Notes should be sent to the Publications Program, Foreign Policy Institute, 1619 Massachusetts Avenue, N.W., Washington, D.C. 20036-2297/(202) 663-5765.